Prayer Answered

in the Backyard

Kay Frances King Munson

Illustrated by John Fraser

All Scripture taken from the New King James Version®,
Copyright © 1982 by Thomas Nelson. Used by permission. All rights reserved.

Copyright © 2016 Kay Frances King Munson
Copyright © 2016 TEACH Services, Inc.
ISBN-13: 978-1-4796-0591-0 (Paperback)
ISBN-13: 978-1-4796-0592-7 (iBooks)
ISBN-13: 978-1-4796-0593-4 (Kindle Fire)
Library of Congress Control No: 2016903867

TEACH Services, Inc.
PUBLISHING
www.TEACHServices.com • (800) 367-1844

Dedication

This book is dedicated to my son, Channing Martell Munson, and to all my children whom I have taught over the years. It is through the eyes of children that I have come to visualize the importance of God's Word. Teaching them how to pray and to have faith, hope, and love.

I pray that as you read this story you will find the joy of discovering Jesus and sharing Him with your family, friends, and others who you encounter.

This story is a testimony to the importance of the seventh-day Sabbath as taught in Genesis 1:1–30. The Sabbath was created by God as a day of worship and rest in memorial of creation week. God's people have kept the Sabbath throughout the Bible.

It was a very hot day in July. The temperature was 100 degrees outside. With sweat pouring down his face, Mr. Cameron was doing his best to start the car so his family could go to church. He had problems with the car before, but this time it wouldn't start no matter how hard he worked on it. His family was so disappointed because they knew they would miss church that Saturday, which is the Cameron's Sabbath, their day of Worship.

The Cameron family lived about five miles outside of Fayetteville, North Carolina. The children loved attending services every Sabbath. Tia was fourteen years old and the oldest of seven children. Tia's brother Channing was twelve years old and a very talkative, creative, and expressive child. He was called the prayer warrior in the family. He loved listening to Pastor Mason preach on Sabbath mornings. He wrote down verses in the sermon so he could memorize them.

Channing said to his father, "Dad, we will pray and ask God to give us another car to get to church."

"Yes," Dad said. "We will have faith and believe God will answer our prayers."

Time passed and the family walked to church when the weather was good or accepted rides from other church members. One family in particular offered to help the Cameron family get to church, but they could only fit five extra people in their car, so Dad took Tia, Channing, Joseph, and Ebony to church while Mom stayed home with the other three children and had church with them. They were thankful for the help, but they still prayed that they could get a car.

One day the family who was supposed to pick them up didn't show up because they had gone out of town. The children were very sad, but Channing was more upset than all the others. Wanting to be alone, he strolled outside to the front yard and slowly walked to the backyard. He saw how beautiful it was outside. The sun shone bright on the grass and the leaves were tinged with different colors, for it was the first day of fall.

Channing loved Sabbath and worshiping God, and he was very disappointed that, once again, he and his family would miss church. He knew he had to do something before sunset. Then, all of a sudden, he got an idea!

He ran into the house and asked Mom if he could wear his dad's choir robe.

She looked a little puzzled at him and said, "What do you want it for, son?"

"Don't worry, Mom, I won't get it dirty. I promise to take good care of it."

"OK, go ahead," Mom said.

Channing called his sisters and brothers to come outside and join him in the backyard, "Let's have church in the backyard today. Let's do everything they do on Sabbath morning at the 11 o'clock service," he said excitedly.

"Hey, that sounds like a fantastic suggestion," Tia said.

"I'll be Pastor Mason," Channing stated.

He already had his dad's robe on, even though it hung down to his feet. His sisters and brothers tried to hold back their laughter as Channing continued to give out instructions.

"I'll be Sister Tillman," Tia interjected. "She inspires me when she reads the Scriptures."

"I'll be Brother King," Joseph said. "His voice is powerful when he prays."

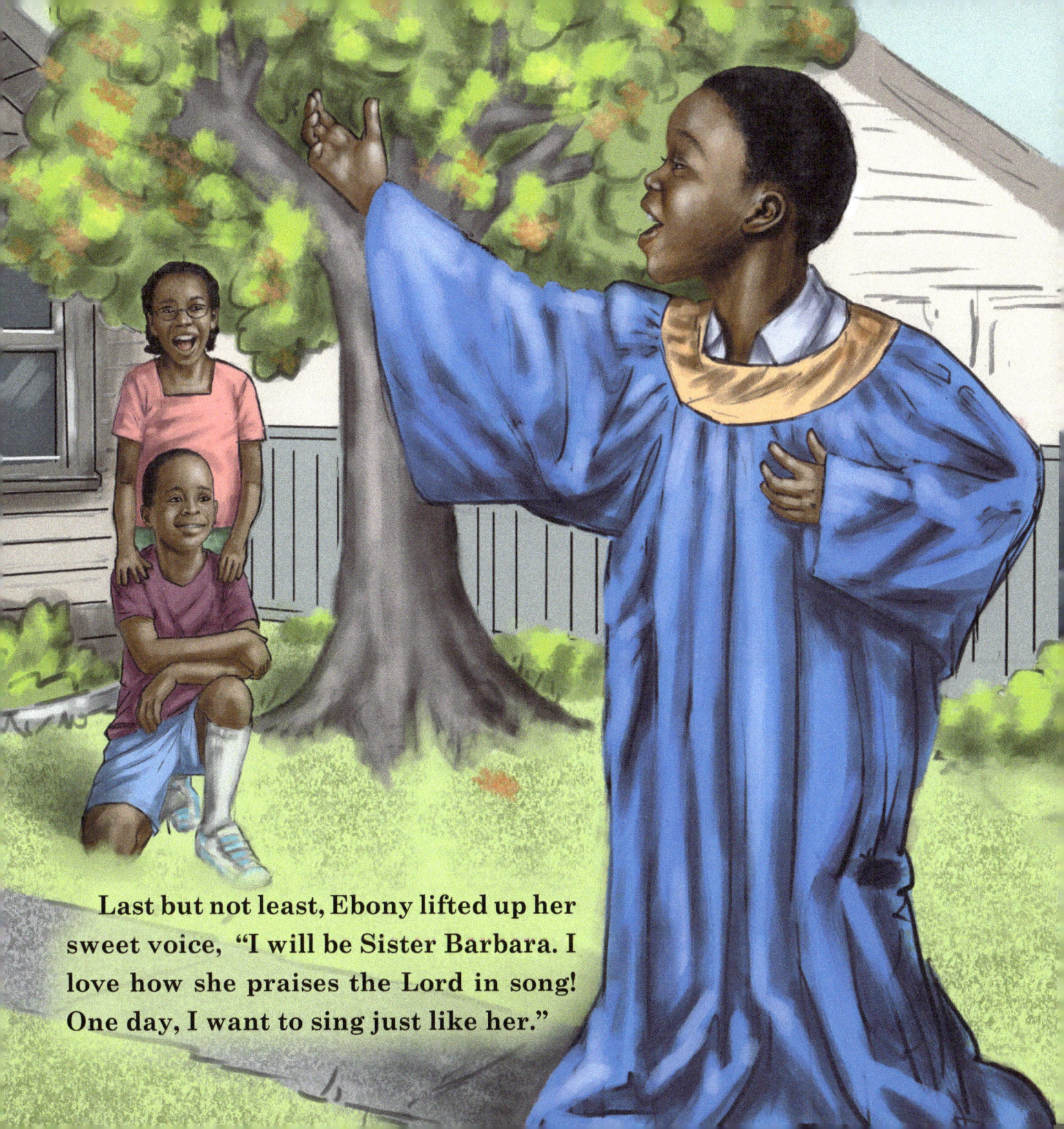

Last but not least, Ebony lifted up her sweet voice, "I will be Sister Barbara. I love how she praises the Lord in song! One day, I want to sing just like her."

The other three children, Tiffany, Grace, and David, ran to the back door when they heard what their brothers and sisters were planning. They ran around excitedly, saying, "We will be the congregation!"

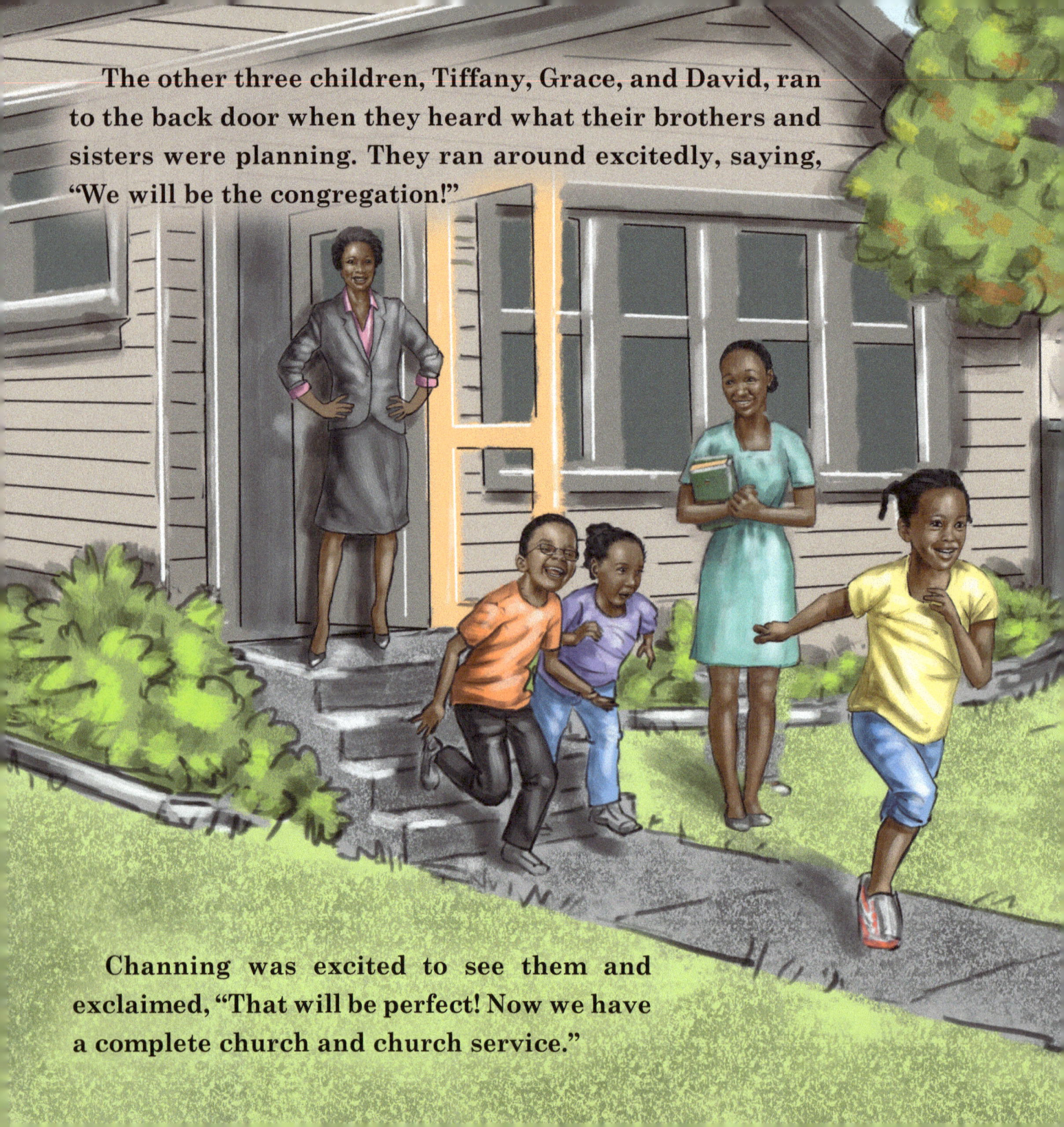

Channing was excited to see them and exclaimed, "That will be perfect! Now we have a complete church and church service."

Mom came to the door, and when she saw Channing, she smiled at the thought that he wanted to be like Pastor Mason. She knew how much the family missed going to church every Sabbath, but she was so proud to see her children worshiping and praising God in their own special way.

When the service began, Ebony sang her little heart out, Tia read the Scripture, Joseph prayed a fervent prayer, and Channing preached. The title of his sermon was, "Lord, We Need a Car Right Now."

At the end of the sermon he prayed, "Lord, I was going to ask You to help Dad get a car, but Lord, we really need a van because there are eight of us. And with Mom and Dad, Lord, that makes ten!"

The children giggled a little when Channing made that statement. He was talking so fast that he had miscounted. Tia whispered to him, "Nine, not ten."

Everybody giggled again but remained reverent while Channing continued his prayer. "Lord, You said You would give us the desires of our heart when we ask in Your name. So Lord, here we are, Your children. We are asking for transportation, a car or van, whatever You can give us so we can get to church as a family to serve You. Please hear our prayer, Lord. Amen."

While Channing was praying, Mr. Evan, their elderly next door neighbor, was listening through the fence. He never spoke to the children or socialized with the Cameron family, but when he heard the children singing and praying loudly, he had come outside to see what on earth was going on.

He heard Channing's request for a car or van to get the family to church and his heart was touched by the sincerity of the boy's prayer. He listened to the children a long time and then went back into his house without saying a word to them.

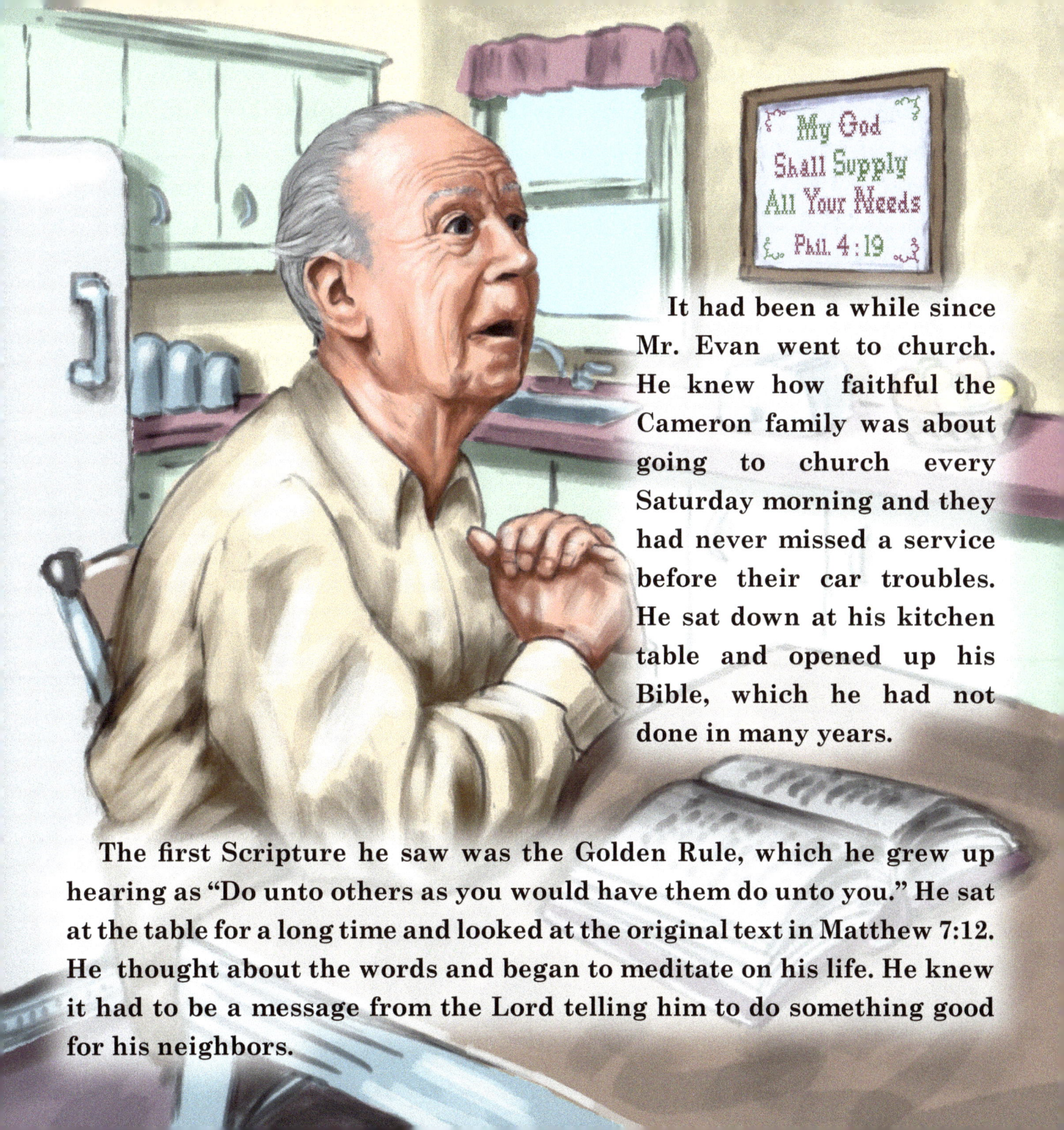

It had been a while since Mr. Evan went to church. He knew how faithful the Cameron family was about going to church every Saturday morning and they had never missed a service before their car troubles. He sat down at his kitchen table and opened up his Bible, which he had not done in many years.

The first Scripture he saw was the Golden Rule, which he grew up hearing as "Do unto others as you would have them do unto you." He sat at the table for a long time and looked at the original text in Matthew 7:12. He thought about the words and began to meditate on his life. He knew it had to be a message from the Lord telling him to do something good for his neighbors.

That evening Mr. Evan rang the doorbell at the Cameron's house. Mr. Cameron answered the door. His family had just closed the Sabbath with Scripture, singing, and prayer. This was their way of giving God the glory for His goodness, mercies, and kindness to them. Channing was very surprised when his dad opened the door and saw Mr. Evan standing there.

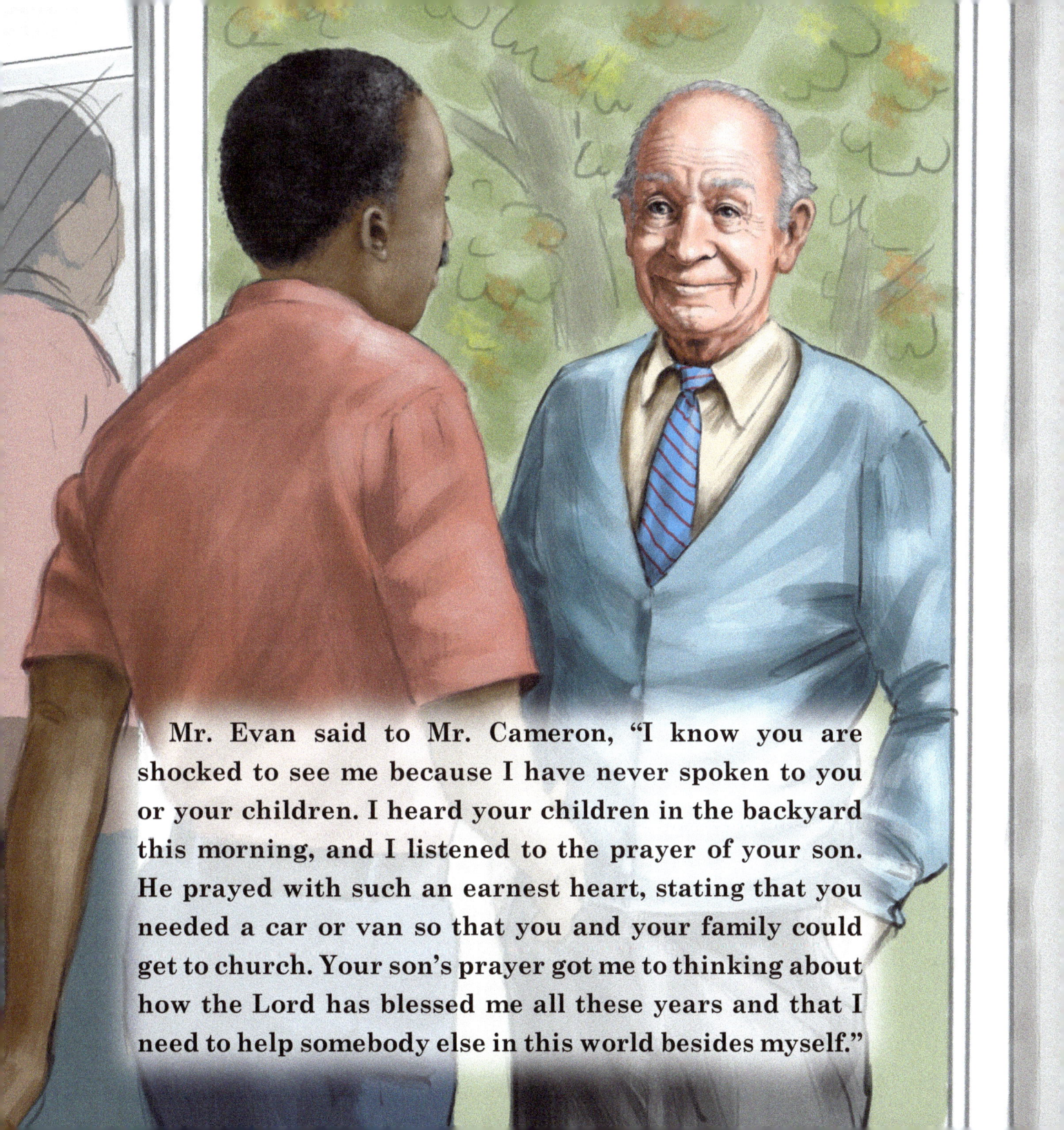

Mr. Evan said to Mr. Cameron, "I know you are shocked to see me because I have never spoken to you or your children. I heard your children in the backyard this morning, and I listened to the prayer of your son. He prayed with such an earnest heart, stating that you needed a car or van so that you and your family could get to church. Your son's prayer got me to thinking about how the Lord has blessed me all these years and that I need to help somebody else in this world besides myself."

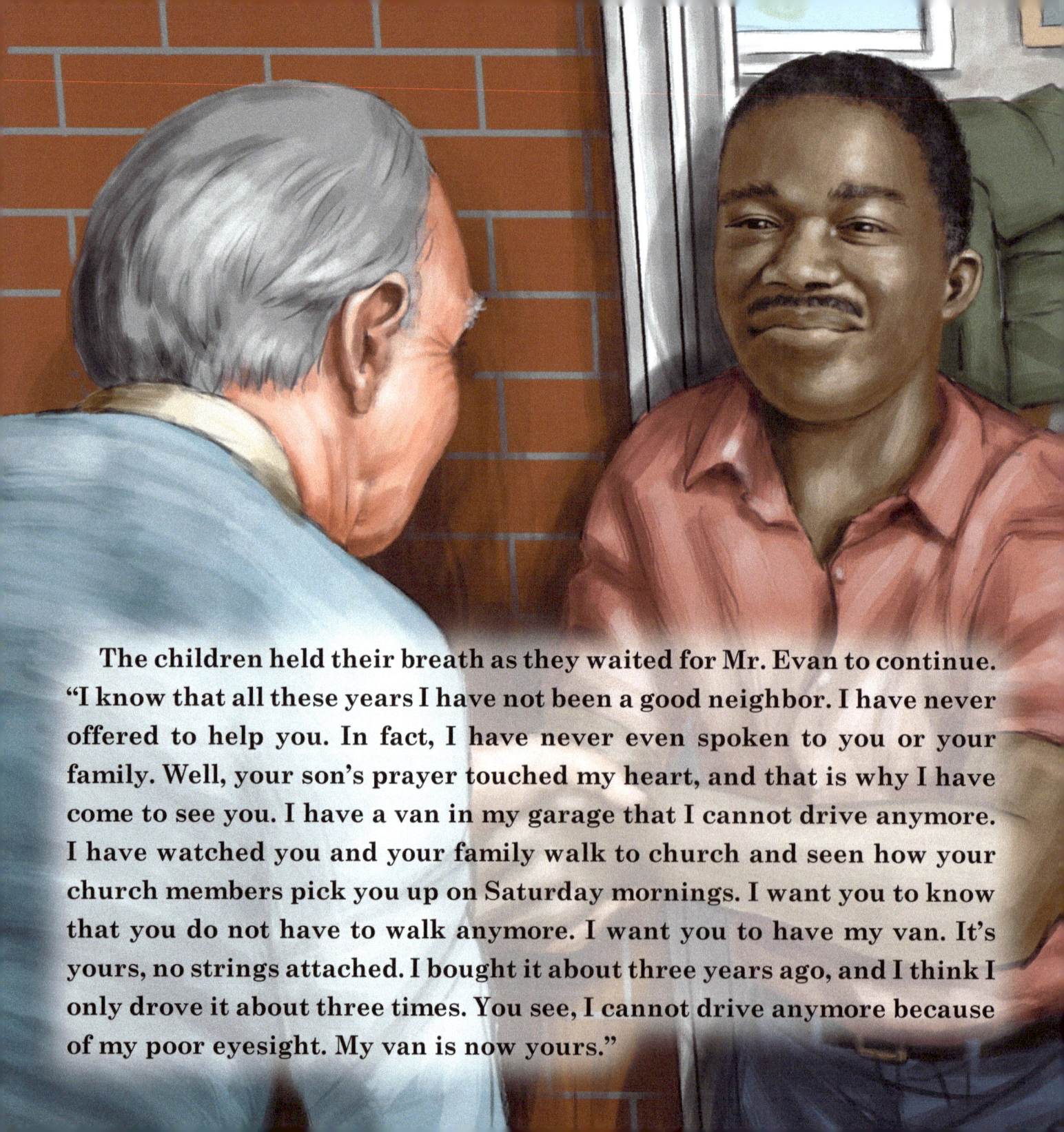

The children held their breath as they waited for Mr. Evan to continue. "I know that all these years I have not been a good neighbor. I have never offered to help you. In fact, I have never even spoken to you or your family. Well, your son's prayer touched my heart, and that is why I have come to see you. I have a van in my garage that I cannot drive anymore. I have watched you and your family walk to church and seen how your church members pick you up on Saturday mornings. I want you to know that you do not have to walk anymore. I want you to have my van. It's yours, no strings attached. I bought it about three years ago, and I think I only drove it about three times. You see, I cannot drive anymore because of my poor eyesight. My van is now yours."

Mr. Cameron was so overjoyed that tears ran down his cheeks. He was speechless and felt wonderfully blessed by the generous gift that Mr. Evan had given to his family.

Mrs. Cameron and the children heard what Mr. Evan had said, and they came running to the door. They jumped up and down, sang, and praised God for answering their prayers.

Channing gave Mr. Evan a firm handshake and thanked him for helping his family. Mr. Cameron invited Mr. Evan to come to church with them anytime he wished, and he accepted with a gracious heart.

Mr. Evan left the house knowing it was God who gave him the courage to show love again. He heard the Cameron family still praising God for his gift. His heart was filled with joy, for he knew for the first time in his life that he had done just what he was supposed to do. He had obeyed the word of the Lord. He had given a gift that a family needed and without reservation.

He was so happy that when he got home he open his Bible again, and the first Scripture he saw was Acts 20:35: "I have shown in every way, by laboring like this, that you must support the weak. And remember the words of the Lord Jesus, that He said, 'It is more blessed to give than to receive.'"

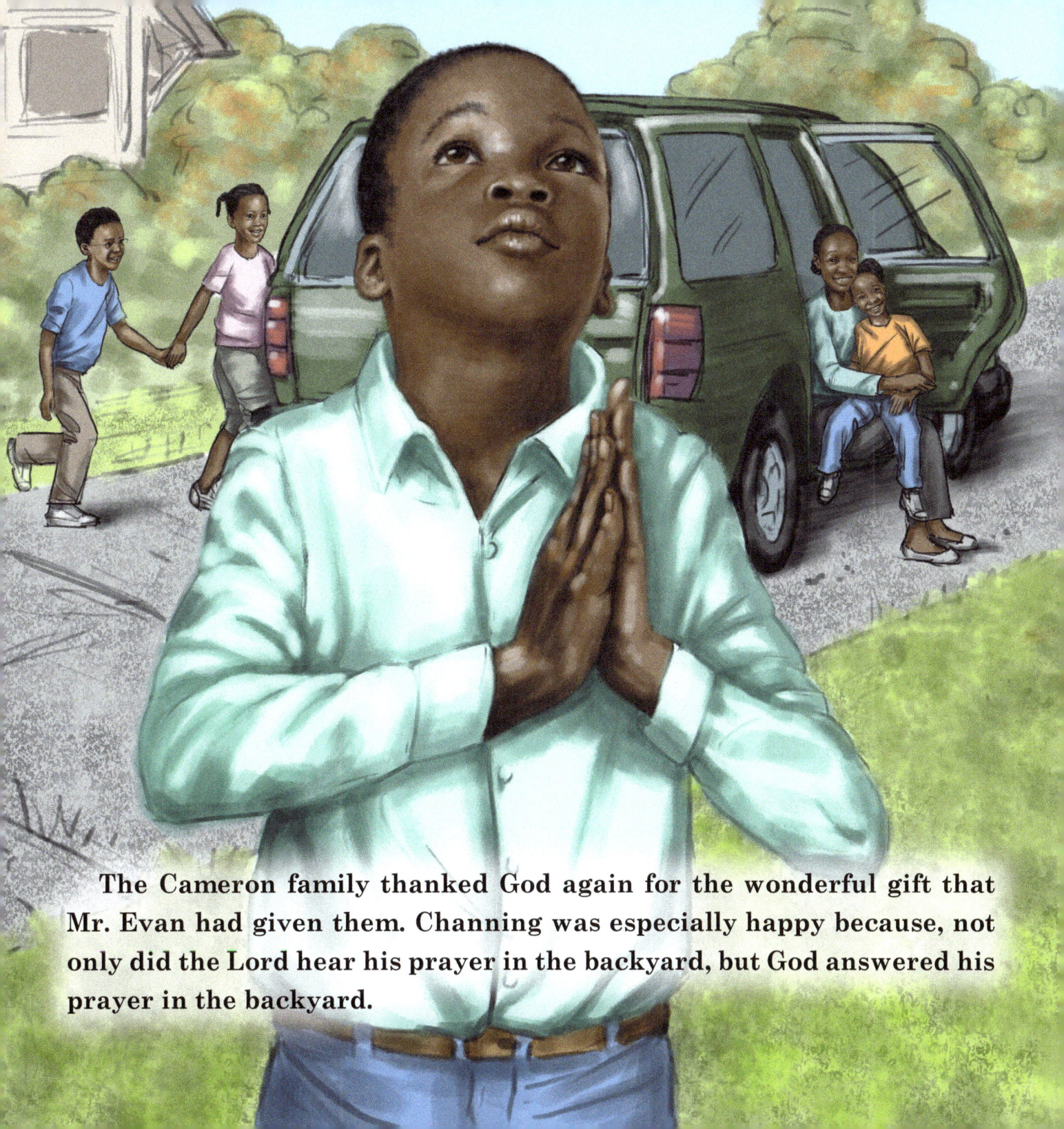

The Cameron family thanked God again for the wonderful gift that Mr. Evan had given them. Channing was especially happy because, not only did the Lord hear his prayer in the backyard, but God answered his prayer in the backyard.

We invite you to view the complete
selection of titles we publish at:

www.TEACHServices.com

Scan with your mobile
device to go directly
to our website.

Please write or e-mail us your praises, reactions, or
thoughts about this or any other book we publish at:

TEACH Services, Inc.
P U B L I S H I N G
www.TEACHServices.com ● (800) 367-1844

P.O. Box 954
Ringgold, GA 30736

info@TEACHServices.com

TEACH Services, Inc., titles may be purchased in bulk for
educational, business, fund-raising, or sales promotional use.
For information, please e-mail:

BulkSales@TEACHServices.com

Finally, if you are interested in seeing
your own book in print, please contact us at

publishing@TEACHServices.com

We would be happy to review your manuscript for free.

www.ingramcontent.com/pod-product-compliance
Lightning Source LLC
Chambersburg PA
CBHW061416090426
42742CB00026B/3489